CW01497530

SACRED FEET YOGA TEACHINGS

SACRED FEET YOGA TEACHINGS

with Meditations by Swami Prakashananda

To my dear friend Heather
with love,
Swami Prakashananda Ji

SACRED  FEET

Sacred Feet Yoga Teachings
with Meditations by Swami Prakashananda

Print ISBN: 978-0-9996800-1-8
EBook ISBN: 978-0-9996800-2-5

Published by SACRED FEET
The Interfaith/Interspiritual/Trans-Theological Publishing Imprint
of The Jones Educational Foundation, Inc. (JEFI) 501 (c) 3 Not-For-Profit Corporation
303 W. Columbia Street, Somerset, KY 42501, USA
www.jefifoundation.org

Printed in the United States of America
First published 2023

SACRED FEET YOGA CREED

We honor the basic truths found in all religions. In our view, truth and dogma are not synonymous, and we do not seek to impose a belief system on practitioners. Ours is a yoga that focuses on sacred energy.

We seek to develop the Christ Spirit or Guru Spirit in those who practice Sacred Feet Yoga. We do not consider any one teacher to be Lord of the Universe but look to all legitimate teachers for wisdom and guidance.

Our major focus is on the Holy Spirit or Maha Kundalini Shakti. It is She who leads us to freedom from the vicissitudes of the human ego. In Sacred Feet Yoga philosophy, freedom is possible in the life we are living if we are willing to work for it.

Jaya Jaya Amrita Guru,
Jaya Shri Jagadguru Namah!

(Praises to the Guru who delivers the delicious spiritual nectar!)

Swami Shraddhananda, (1948 – 2021)
Founder of Sacred Feet Yoga
Dec. 30, 2020

"Wisdom is brilliant, she never fades. By those who love her, she is readily seen, by those who seek her, she is readily found. She anticipates those who desire her by making herself known first. Whoever gets up early to seek her will have no trouble but will find her sitting at the door.

Meditating on her is understanding in its perfect form, and anyone keeping awake for her will soon be free from care.

For she herself searches everywhere for those who are worthy of her, benevolently appearing to them on their ways, anticipating their every thought."

— Book of Wisdom 6:12-16

"*Om purnamidam.*
Praises to my true blue Guru
on Guru Purnima.
From her true blue disciple."

— Swami Shraddhananda ("Mataji")

Dedicated with much love and gratitude,
to the memory of Swami Shraddhananda Saraswati,
Founder of Sacred Feet Yoga

May all seekers everywhere awaken to the Divine within.
May the grace inherent in these Teachings bestow Liberation.

Sw. Shraddhananda with Shiva Nataraj
Anugraha House, Somerset, KY, USA

TABLE OF CONTENTS

SACRED FEET YOGA LINEAGE   i
THREE DHARMA HEIRS   iii
FOREWORD   iv

SACRED FEET YOGA TEACHINGS — LEVEL ONE   1

MEDITATIONS
1.1.1 — Be as kind to yourself as you are compassionate to others.   2
1.1.2 — Be as forgiving of yourself as you are generous with others.   3
1.1.3 — Be as patient with yourself as you are faithful to others.   4
1.2.1 — Trust yourself.   5
1.2.2 — Trust in your own deep heart.   6
1.2.3 — Trust in the dance of the universe.   7
1.3.1 — Honor the sacred energy at the core of your being.   8
1.3.2 — Nurture the Holy Spirit's bright and faithful fire.   9
1.3.3 — Digest the knowledge that leads unfailingly to freedom.   10
1.4.1 — Live your life peacefully—and with purpose.   11
1.4.2 — Maintain a glad sense of humor.   12
1.4.3 — Place your faith in stillness, steadiness and service.   13
1.5.1 — Be gentle and fair in your dealings.   14
1.5.2 — Praise others and receive praise graciously.   15
1.5.3 — Be a courier of faith and wakefulness.   16

SACRED FEET YOGA TEACHINGS — LEVEL TWO   17

MEDITATIONS
2.1.1 — Practice self-inquiry.   18
2.1.2 — Expose your egoic projections.   19
2.1.3 — Uproot your time-honored narratives.   20
2.2.1 — Loosen your hold on lack.   21
2.2.2 — Discern between love and need.   22
2.2.3 — Let go of constriction and contrition.   23
2.3.1 — Cooperate with purification.   24
2.2.2 — Study the sacred energy commentaries.   25
2.2.3 — Memorize the vibrations of sacred energy in your body.   26
2.4.1 — Open to your deepest wisdom.   27
2.4.2 — Place your greatness in the light.   28
2.4.3 — Welcome your team of guides.   29
2.5.1 — Focus on courage.   30
2.5.2 — Partner with liberation, your own, other beings, the earth.   31
2.5.3 — Be constant in your quest to live in an enlightened state.   32

MEDITATIONS

3.1.1 — Sacred is everywhere.   34
3.1.2 — Discern the path to your sacred feet.   35
3.1.3 — Grace does not make mistakes.   36
3.2.1 — Abide in the breath.   37
3.2.2 — Abide in your own deep heart.   38
3.2.3 — Abide in the nectar of *purno'ham*, completeness.   39
3.3.1 — Let go of ego's concerns.   40
3.3.2 — Release all expectations.   41
3.3.3 — Dissolve the fear of separation.   42
3.4.1 — Reboot in every moment.   43
3.4.2 — Listen with attention.   44
3.4.3 — Be happy; revel in the joy of being.   45
3.5.1 — Recognize the Divine Essence in all.   46
3.5.2 — Serve unconditionally. Love all, reject none.   47
3.5.3 — Merge in the heart of the universe.   48

FURTHER READING   49

SACRED FEET YOGA LINEAGE

The lineage of Sacred Feet Yoga stretches back into time immemorable, with its roots in the tradition of the great Siddhas, enlightened Masters being too many to count, with many hidden from the public eye.

Bhagavan Nityananda (Died 1961)

In the early 20th Century, the great Indian Saint, Shri Bhagavan Nityananda of Ganeshpuri, emerged as an *Avadhut,* a fully enlightened being. He spent his early years as a wandering monk and eventually settled down in Kanhangad, Kerala, India, establishing his first ashram there. In later years, he moved to Ganeshpuri, a village in Maharashtra, India, establishing another ashram there. It became his final resting place. Thousands of people from all over the world came to visit and receive Bhagavan's blessings, including India's many saints. India's top Government Ministers often sought out his advice. In spite of his fame, he lived in a completely non-attached state, owning nothing, living in the utmost simplicity. Bhagavan Nityananda was that rare being who was always in the ecstatic state of Conscious Awareness. When he did occasionally speak, his teachings were cryptic, but most received everything directly through his state of pure silence.

Swami Shraddhananda (1948 – 2021)

A Successor in the lineage of Shri Bhagavan Nityananda of Ganeshpuri, Swami Shraddhananda was a highly regarded Spiritual Teacher who studied with key enlightened teachers of classical tantra for thirty years. In earlier years, Swami

Shraddhananda was known in academic circles as Rev. Dr. Sonya L. Jones.

As Dr. Jones, she offered her service for 35 years in the academic world as Professor of the Classics, World Literature, and Comparative World Religions, and as first Dean of Graduate Studies at The New Seminary, New York City, the oldest Interfaith institution in the world.

In 2010, she co-founded The Jones Educational Foundation, Inc., the organization headquartered in Somerset, Kentucky (USA) that administers Sacred Feet Yoga. Two years later, she was initiated into the Saraswati Order of Monastics in Ganeshpuri, India, and subsequently, as lineage holder and Preceptor for The Community of the Mystic Heart, an Interspiritual monastic group founded by Brother Wayne Teasdale.

In later years, her close students called her by the endearment "Mataji," which means "Respected Mother." In 2010, Mataji received The Five Teachings of Sacred Feet Yoga Level One by transmission from her Siddha guides. She received a second transmission of Sacred Feet Yoga Teachings in 2017.

The spine of Sacred Feet Yoga rests in The Third Teachings of Level One which encourage seekers to open to *Shaktipat,* the awakening of the Sacred Energy known as *Maha Kundalini Shakti*, or the Holy Spirit.

Sacred Feet Yoga is also embodied through Hatha Yoga practice where students imbibe the Teachings into the very tissues of the body as the words are spoken aloud or whispered internally.

The Teachings of Sacred Feet Yoga continue to evolve. At Mataji's transition in February of 2021, Swami Prakashananda received a transmission of a third level of Teachings to augment the first two levels. All three levels of Sacred Feet Yoga Teachings are included in this book.

THREE DHARMA HEIRS

Swami Shraddhananda's work is continued by her three appointed Dharma Heirs. Each one is a successor in the lineage of Bhagavan Nityananda of Ganeshpuri, India, offering spiritual awakening (*Shaktipat*) and guidance.

In the USA:

Acharya Sandra (Chamatkara) Simon, Dharma Heir located in Pittsburgh, PA, was the first appointed Senior Acharya (Senior Teacher) in Sacred Feet Yoga by Swami Shraddhananda. She currently serves as President for The Jones Educational Foundation, Inc. and has overall responsibility as Manager and Editor-in-Chief of The Sacred Feet Publishing Imprint. Sandra can be contacted at sandrajsimon@hotmail.com.

Acharya Jenny (Amrita) Williams, Dharma Heir located in Somerset, KY at Anugraha House, was appointed by Swami Shraddhananda as a Senior Acharya and serves with a special focus on Hatha Yoga Teachings. Jenny also serves as Vice President for The Jones Educational Foundation, Inc. and can be contacted at jennyannharness@gmail.com.

Sacred Feet Yoga/JEFI HQ Mailing Address: Anugraha House, 303 W. Columbia St., Somerset, KY 42501

Serving Europe and the Rest of the World:

Swami Prakashananda, Dharma Heir located in the United Kingdom, was initiated by Swami Shraddhananda into the traditional Saraswati order of Indian monks and into the lineage of Br. Wayne Teasdale with the Community of the Mystic Heart. She was appointed as a Senior Acharya with a special focus on Sacred Teachings. She also serves as a Bishop in the Independent Sacramental Movement, where she is better known as the Rt. Rev. Chris Deefholts. Her Ministry is especially focused on the awakening and unfolding of the Holy Spirit. Swamiji can be contacted at swprakashji@gmail.com.

FOREWORD

During the course of her ministry, in 2010 and again in 2017, Swami Shraddhananda (Mataji) received a direct transmission of spiritual teachings from her team of Siddha Guides, Sages and Teachers, Saints that reside in and teach through the subtle realms. These Sacred Feet Yoga Teachings are veritable treasures that have supported hundreds of students in the ensuing years. They are presented here with the Meditations that she commissioned me to write with some urgency, just before she made her transition, with the request that they be offered out initially in digital form and subsequently in print.

Mataji also referred to a third level of Teachings that were originally intended for sannyasins, but which did not materialise during her lifetime. This third level was transmitted by my team of Siddha guides at the significant time of Mataji's passing in February of 2021. Given the challenges of the present time, it was recognised by all three Dharma Heirs that the Level Three Teachings of Sacred Feet Yoga should be offered out to *all* sincere seekers to support them on the spiritual journey and to help them anchor in the enlightened state. As such, they have been included in this book as well with accompanying Meditations.

There are so many divine souls, both seen and unseen, that have contributed to enabling the fruition of this book—too many to mention by name—but, in particular, I should like to salute my Spiritual Teachers along the path, Mataji herself—our Spiritual Preceptor, and my two shining sister Co-Dharma Heirs, Jenny (Amrita) Williams and Sandra (Chamatkara) Simon. I also offer my gratitude to the wonderful Lyn Devi Parkinson, who wholeheartedly believed in this project and offered her time and encouragement from beginning to end. My deep bow of thanks to you all.

May these Teachings open the spiritual door for you, and may you become anchored in the awareness of the scintillating Divine Heart, the golden vibration of Consciousness upholding every experience.

— Swami Prakashananda
Co-Dharma Heir, Sacred Feet Yoga
(Pentecost 2023)

SACRED FEET YOGA TEACHINGS
LEVEL ONE

The First Teachings
1. Be as kind to yourself as you are compassionate to others.
2. Be as forgiving of yourself as you are generous with others.
3. Be as patient with yourself as you are faithful to others.

The Second Teachings
1. Trust yourself.
2. Trust in your own deep heart.
3. Trust in the dance of the universe.

The Third Teachings
1. Honor the sacred energy at the core of your being.
2. Nurture the Holy Spirit's bright and faithful fire.
3. Digest the knowledge that leads unfailingly to freedom.

The Fourth Teachings
1. Live your life peacefully—and with purpose.
2. Maintain a glad sense of humor.
3. Place your faith in stillness, steadiness and service.

The Fifth Teachings
1. Be gentle and fair in your dealings.
2. Praise others and receive praise graciously.
3. Be a courier of faith and wakefulness.

Received by Rev. Dr. Sonya L. Jones, Ma Bhavani Brahmacharya (later initiated as Swami Shraddhananda), from her team of Siddha guides (June 24 – July 5, 2010)

TEACHING 1.1.1

Be as kind to yourself as you are compassionate to others.

The first three teachings of Sacred Feet Yoga invite us to reflect deeply on the impact of our behaviours and attitudes from the aspect of relationship—with ourselves and with others. Our reactions can seesaw, become over-balanced in one direction and impoverished or unconsidered in another.

Self-regulation is a practice that has been cultivated for centuries in the name of spirituality, and it is a first step in taming the outer senses. However, many a time, those on the spiritual path offer kindness and compassion to others and yet forget to include themselves, or perhaps even reject or deprive themselves out of a sense of unworthiness. Consider that self-control is not the same as self-repression.

For a seeker to mature and appreciate the more subtle self-aware states, one must include oneself in the equation and set aside the ego tendency to put oneself down. Such self-denial is an expression of the personality, the strong ego that keeps us locked in a state of separation from the experience of our essential nature.

Can we step aside, observe our responses, and hold the inner balance? As we express kindness towards ourselves, know that the quality of kindness arises from ourselves and radiates out to others. In the same way, as we express compassion in our thoughts and actions, recognise that this quality arises from ourselves and that we bathe in the same attribute as we express it.

How might this first Teaching be helpfully applied in our everyday lives in dealing with, say, work issues? Selfless service in the community? In our family structures?

TEACHING 1.1.2

Be as forgiving of yourself as you are generous with others.

Forgiveness arises when we can acknowledge our humanity and our mistakes. When we have remorse for our actions and thoughts, and compassionate understanding, then we can harvest the lessons that arise from our mistakes and move forward in wisdom.

Mistakes are the mechanism through which human beings evolve. Even an innocent, thought-free child will topple over when learning to grapple with new concepts like walking and speech. With self-acceptance, children pick themselves up and begin their practice for self-mastery again. As the Master Jesus once advised, "Be as little children."

Forgiveness arises from empathy—we learn to walk in another's shoes and show compassion and generosity towards others.

Can we accept ourselves, too, and learn to walk with equanimity and peace in our own shoes, on our own path? Can we own our mistakes and allow ourselves to fall open to grace? To the inner guiding wisdom? Such intimacy with ourselves is an essential requirement if we wish to free ourselves of unnecessary habits and old recurring patterns. Can we rise to meet these obscuring tendencies and recognise them for what they are?

Carry this Teaching around with you as you walk through your day. Allow insights to arise as you reflect. Let the Teaching reverse itself. Be as generous with yourself as you are forgiving to others. Are you generous with yourself? Are you too generous? Too forbidding? Avoid any judgement. This is an opportunity for discernment and self-revelation.

You may find it a helpful practice to note down your reflections in a journal dedicated for the purpose.

TEACHING 1.1.3

Be as patient with yourself as you are faithful to others.

The experience of all the great saints states that the kingdom of heaven is within and that the wholeness we seek lies there. They say that the greatest challenge of our lifetime is to undertake this sacred journey of discovery for ourselves.

The great sages teach that the experience of everything arises from our deepest core, our essential nature, that is, the Divine consciousness that continuously expresses through all our individual vehicles.

Nature plays with us. The sense of duality, contraction, enables us to function in our physical world, and we learn as children to identify with the separate parts. Most of us eventually lose our sense of wholeness. And yet, like individual bees, we are all part of the same dancing consciousness. The phenomenon of differences is always arising from within our own being, and we unconsciously project our impressions onto others.

How delightful it is to see all the positive attributes that we radiate being reflected in another, as in a mirror! How humbling, too, to realise that all the disowned attributes, the ones we see reflected in others, are also dormant within. Can we be patient with ourselves as we learn to own all our separate parts whilst we slowly dissolve our sense of separation from another, from the cosmic collective?

Faith arises from our direct experience; it is not a matter of accepting another's opinion, which ultimately, is just not enough. We must find out for ourselves!

May your journey be supported by grace and the wisdom gained from direct experience, and may your patience lead you into Divine awareness.

Seated Buddha, Somerset, KY, USA

TEACHING 1.2.1

Trust yourself.

Trusting is fundamental to our development. Once we begin to separate from our mothers and look outside our family unit, we tend to look elsewhere for reassurance, for making our decisions, and for determining our direction. Trusting ourselves may require listening and discernment to distinguish between the layers of different experiences and attitudes that colour our judgement on the one hand and, on the other, the clear inner voice which truly reflects what we know.

This journey within may need courage to recognise that we don't always know with certainty that the decisions we make in life are the right ones for us. At times, we may feel wobbly, like an athlete learning to balance on a rope. In the beginning, we are aware that we might topple over, yet place our confidence in our ability to learn and in our practice to support us and to make us strong. We trust that the mistakes we make along the way strengthen us through the lessons we learn. We learn that whilst we may receive responses to our questions, the answers arise from within.

At some point, we realise that skillful help may be really useful. We might decide to take the support of a good Teacher for a while as we learn to navigate the more subtle aspects of our path. The function of such a Teacher is to open locked doors and to offer support as we walk through, like a mother offering a hand when a child is learning to walk.

A Teacher might suggest a spiritual practice that develops trust in oneself or a challenging task that helps the student to recognise underdeveloped or unacknowledged qualities within themselves or unhelpful attitudes which slow down progress, stepping back as the student develops deep trust in grace and in the Teacher within themselves.

TEACHING 1.2.2

Trust in your own deep heart.

In everyday life, we often check with others, receiving a variety of opinions. We might reject some of those replies outright whilst others might be recognised as having value and generate a response in us. Ultimately though, the real answer to a question or situation will leap forth from within our own deep heart once it is recognised.

Our own deep heart is our innermost core, the state of awareness that is our Divine essence. It is known by many names: the Inner Light, God within, Divine Consciousness, the Self (with a capital "S"), and the inner Teacher principle or guide within our own being that we connect with through our own direct experience.

Through regularly practicing meditation, we develop our observation skills. We learn discernment. We discover the layers of conditioning that distort our perceptions and the personal experiences and preferences that sway our decisions.

We also begin to experience the different states of consciousness that arise as the body and mind become steady and still. The waking state reflects our body connection whilst in the dream state, the mind is still active. In deep sleep, the body and mind are at rest.

Letting go of the thought waves allows us to pass through the deep sleep state and into the profound silence and clarity of the supra causal or *turiya* state. It is this state of awareness that lies at the core of our being, our true nature which underlies and sustains all our functions and which is always awake.

As we practice trusting in our own deep heart, our attention becomes increasingly aligned and anchored in Truth.

TEACHING 1.2.3

Trust in the dance of the universe.

There is an inherent quality of playfulness to Divine Consciousness, which lies at the root of every thought, action, and reality. In fact, our whole universe of names and forms emerges out of the initial primal pulsation in the same way that the underlying primary coding on a computer supports the production of a personal letter on the screen or a complicated program. It is very easy to get lost in the dramas and identities in which we find ourselves, and to get drawn into the alluring kaleidoscope of stories running through our lives. We forget that we are, indeed, Supreme Consciousness playing a role. We are all Lords and Ladies participating in the dance of the life that is our playground.

Trust enables us to greet the challenges of life wholeheartedly and brings out our courage. When we get caught up in seemingly impossible situations, it is by trusting in the universal dance that we can move forward. Then, whatever happens, we are fully supported by the grace of the Holy Spirit, aka *Maha Kundalini Shakti*. Even our mistakes and difficulties turn into gold and become divine gifts that help us to grow in understanding and joy. By handing each situation over to the deeper wisdom within us, we gradually become lighter in spirit, and our awareness becomes more and more anchored in our essential nature.

There is an old gospel song that says: "Give me joy in my heart, keep me praising… keep me praising till the break of day." Maintaining a positive attitude is a great spiritual practice which dispels our darkness, uplifts our whole being, and helps us to practice trust in the universe. This is the path to liberation.

May our awareness remain anchored in the Divine within, whatever else is going on around us!

Shiva Nataraj, Anugraha House, Somerset, KY, USA

TEACHING 1.3.1

Honor the sacred energy at the core of your being.

This third section of the Teachings, which touches on the awakening of the sacred energy that normally lies dormant within each one of us, is considered to be the spine of Sacred Feet Yoga. It also considers the way in which we enable the sacred energy to work effectively through us.

The Sacred Energy at the core of your being is recognised in many spiritual traditions and goes by many names, such as Windhorse, *Kundalini Shakti*, the Holy Spirit, the Comforter... She is the electricity that lights up the seeker's house. She is grace in action.

There comes a moment in our lives when we yearn for completeness, and this initiates an awakening which reveals our essential nature. Yogis call it *Shaktipat,* which means "the descent of grace." The Holy Spirit may occasionally awaken spontaneously, but the safest way to activate the sacred energy, that is, to receive *Shaktipat,* is through someone who knows how to work with it: that may be a Buddhist Lama, a *Shaktipat* Guru, a mystical Rabbi or Sufi Sheikh—or a Christian or Interfaith Minister.

One may also safely receive *Shaktipat* through the Sacred Feet Yoga tradition. Swami Shraddhananda, the Founder of Sacred Feet Yoga, said of the Holy Spirit: "She sanctifies, empowers, and sets us free from the needs we think we must satisfy for happiness to arrive from distant provinces, when, as a long-time practitioner of Yoga said, *happiness happens inside.*"

To honour the sacred energy, sit quietly and invite the Holy Spirit into your life. The Holy Spirit tends to speak to us and through us when the mind is still and receptive. She will unfailingly lead you back to the core of your own being.

TEACHING 1.3.2

Nurture the Holy Spirit's bright and faithful fire.

When we are lovingly building a fire in the hearth, we prepare it well. We lay the foundations and add suitable kindling. Once the spark is offered, we protect and nourish the flame. We feed it the right kind of food and don't swamp it. We take our time. We watch it establish and let it grow into maturity. It is the same with our own inner fire. How can we nourish and protect the new flame while it is being established?

Sacred Feet Yoga offers us sound and well tested practices such as *seva* (selfless service) as well as specific hatha yoga practices to accompany the Teachings at each stage. These help the student to develop steadiness, self-reflection, and inner strength, enabling them to embody and anchor the Teachings.

The support of chanting, mantra repetition, and regular meditation, together with keeping good company (*Satsang*), allow the seeker to develop discernment and patience. These practices open us to the natural inner joy in our hearts and enable us to venture deeper into the states of our own being. Building the fire often takes us back to first principles such as a positive approach in our behaviour, gentle healthy discipline, and regularity in our lives. Without discipline, regularity, and nurturing support, even our hearts cannot offer us life.

Pay attention to which activities nurture you and which drain your energy or draw you into negativity. Are you sleeping well and regularly? Discover which nourishing foods and activities sustain your meditation practice and which detract. If you are able, set aside a dedicated space for hatha yoga/meditation and a regular time. In this way, meditation will continue throughout your day even when you are unable to practice formally.

TEACHING 1.3.3

Digest the knowledge that leads unfailingly to freedom.

As we steadily continue to build our inner fire, wisdom begins to bubble up from within. The Holy Spirit initially gives us glimpses of our innate essence as we continue our spiritual journey. The Holy Spirit is a purificatory fire that highlights and consumes our repetitive and well-established tendencies (*samskaras*) that generate our sense of suffering and disconnection from the Divine. As the Holy Spirit cleans the inner mirror, it will gradually consume all that is unnecessary. Our faulty thinking and old stories fall away. What used to be regarded as heavy situations will be understood as the Divine means for knowing ourselves better.

We bow to and acknowledge whatever arises and whomever crosses our path, understanding that we digest the knowledge by engaging in the journey of life. Many times, our outer circumstances will dissolve once our attachments are released. Karma falls away. Sometimes, this cleansing can take the form of inner heat or cold sensations, bodily movements, inner visions of past encounters, and other phenomena arising from the subtle body. Don't hold on to these experiences, ecstatic or otherwise, but allow them all to dissolve in the Holy Spirit's bright fire.

In time, we see the inner light shining steadily forth and recognise our inner essence for the core that we truly are, the innate flowing of unity consciousness which is inclusive of all beings and phenomena. We become established in our full awareness as the fire itself, the beacon in the midst of our daily activities that lights up and nourishes all in our local communities. This fullness is the real wisdom. Then, we can wholeheartedly declare, in the joy of freedom, *Ham Sah*! I AM THAT! And *Purno'ham*! I AM COMPLETE!

Shiva's Foot on Apasmara (Embodiment of Ignorance)
Shiva Nataraj, Anugraha House, Somerset, KY, USA

TEACHING 1.4.1

Live your life peacefully and with purpose.

When we "live our life," we have a positive approach where we are the active participant, and it points us in the direction of awakening. Babies naturally dwell in this realm. They are all born with an innate primary awareness, over which they acquire layers of identity and experiences, both good and bad, which help them to anchor into the physical world. As time goes by, we forget our essential nature and identify instead with the overlay of ego and personal stories.

There comes a moment in life when the discomfort becomes so great that we take some first step to take the runaway train in hand. There may be a cry for help, or a firm resolution to begin again. At this point, grace comes winging in to support us. The reboot of *Shaktipat*, the awakening of the Holy Spirit, gives us a reference point to check back on.

We start to distinguish between what is true and what is an overlay. Once we can recognise our coping mechanisms, ego strategies, and emotional reactions for what they are, we can begin to let them go. One great practice for dealing with this clutter is *japa*, the repetition of a mantra.

The effect is to open the door that returns us to the present moment and anchors us there. One can use the above Teaching as *japa* or take an empowered mantra that your Teacher has given to you, repeating it quietly throughout the day whilst going about daily activities.

In this way, we allow ourselves to fall into the natural peace of the Divine within. Those who become adept at peaceful living become contented. They embody this Teaching and radiate it out in their community.

TEACHING 1.4.2

Maintain a glad sense of humor.

In days of old, across the royal courts of Europe, one of the key members of any noble gathering was the presence of the State Fool. What did he do? He maintained a glad sense of humor. He kept the mood of the crowd light, often transforming it at times of great tension. He also acted as a mirror and Conscience for his patron, the only one who was tolerated and free to challenge unaligned behaviour. For those on the spiritual journey, freeing oneself from the tyranny of unconscious tendencies is an essential task.

Humor has been discovered as a wonderful antidote to the heaviness of the ego, so for that reason, in Sacred Feet Yoga, we are encouraged to cultivate lightness of spirit willingly and wholeheartedly. Scientists discovered that when we laugh, the thymus gland, the regulator of our physical health, expands in size, effectively strengthening our immune systems.

Humor, then, is healthy maintenance for our body and for our soul! Laughing at our misconceptions, self-deception, and stories helps us to keep our perspective in balance as well as anchor ourselves into the core of our being.

Maintaining a glad sense of humor is a powerful practice that quickly draws us into the present moment and straight into the heart of Divine Consciousness itself.

Over time, that inner joy becomes a permanent gift which we can readily access at any time for both ourselves and others. Children and liberated beings alike live in the expansive lightness of the Self, unfettered by status or self-image. Their radiant smiles are contagious, spreading a ripple of laughter and well-being.

Radiant Sun, Somerset, KY, USA

TEACHING 1.4.3

Place your faith in stillness, steadiness and service.

Placing our faith requires setting our intention with conviction, with full trust in the Divine that these qualities will serve us well on our spiritual journey.

Stillness is a skill developed through observation and attention. When we identify those ideas and behaviours that draw our focus away from the core of our being, then we can begin to bring the focus back again. In time, we learn to make stillness our permanent residence.

Steadiness is a quality we develop with the firm intention to not get swayed by the ups and downs of life. Instead, we learn to remain anchored in the stillness of the peaceful heart.

The ride in the chariot of life can be a rough one, but when we step back from the sense of "doer-ship" and allow the Divine to take the reins and steer the chariot, then we have protection and guidance. In Sacred Feet Yoga, we often talk about this as "holding our seat."

Selfless service (also known as *seva*) is held to be one of the key spiritual practices for cultivating self-awareness. Whether service is presented as a specific task, or our regular daily work is considered as our practice, nothing is more guaranteed to coordinate body, mind, and soul. At the heart of service is the attitude of offering, and whilst deceptively simple, this practice is very subtle and has many facets.

Above all, selfless service is a journey of self-discovery which expands our focus and enables us to recognise the Divine inherent in everything. Together, stillness, steadiness and service lead us into the silent joy of the heart, the very fabric of everything we do and are.

TEACHING 1.5.1

Be gentle and fair in your dealings.

This Sacred Feet Teaching is clearly a code of behaviour, like a spiritual signpost that points in a helpful direction. One might interpret it as: "Follow the Dharma!" Or perhaps: "Do as you would be done by."

Being fair means treating another with equality and respect, and it implies non-competitiveness. It implies righteousness and appreciation of the "other" and their needs. It implies consideration, the respecting of boundaries and the observing of self-discipline and that everyone's needs have validity.

Children have an innate sense of fairness and sharing, which is eventually overlaid by the development of a more keenly developed sense of individuality.

As adults, we usually have to reboot our programming. Gentleness and kindness act as great antidotes to the aggressive and defensive behaviour that usually abounds in the adult world of commerce and social relationships. Being gentle and fair in our dealings is an ethical stance with a win-win outcome. It addresses the law of balance where, for every action, there is an eventual reaction.

This Sacred Feet Yoga Teaching thus neutralises the selfishness of greed, of taking more than we need. In this way, we keep our footprint light on this Earth. Most actions do, after all, come back to bite us, for good or for bad. Indeed, we eventually eat the fruit of everything we generate. In addition, this practice becomes a soothing balm for our own minds. We become kinder and gentler with ourselves. By embodying the qualities of gentleness and fairness, we receive a great gift, becoming a beacon that radiates out into the world.

TEACHING 1.5.2

Praise others and receive praise graciously.

Praising others is a natural human characteristic. Our ancient seers and sages expressed a natural urge to praise and to glorify Creation through prayers and chanting, and praise was recognised as being significant not just for oneself, but also for the well-being of the whole community. Such powerful praise was thought to change Nature herself and to generate rich crops and rain.

Today, childhood studies show that praise is deeply connected with nurture and the ability to thrive. Even in adult life, encouragement from others helps us to persist in mastering new tasks and in accomplishing difficult endeavours.

This can be said not only for humans but also for any of the higher animals. It has been established by medical experiments that self-perception can mar or maximize early learning and development throughout life. This discovery has immense, wide-reaching implications for our spiritual paths, where we are consciously working on undoing or unhooking from misconceived and received notions about ourselves.

Whilst we may be at ease with giving praise, the ability to receive grace is often a challenge. When we practice receiving praise graciously, it allows us to release old paradigms such as unworthiness and smallness. We develop the capacity to open and to make space for the fullness of the blessing and insight bestowed on us. In this way, we grow in acceptance and recognition of our own Divine greatness.

Therefore, offering and receiving praise is a deeply empowering practice. Both the one who offers praise and the one who receives benefit tremendously from its transformative effects.

TEACHING 1.5.3

Be a courier of faith and wakefulness.

This Sacred Feet Yoga Teaching gives us a blueprint practice for *sadhana*, our spiritual path, which naturally culminates as the full radiance of being.

At a very basic level, a courier is a message bearer, a conveyer, or guide. On a deeper level, couriers embody the purity of the teachings with absolute clarity. They are awakened souls, wisdom carriers radiating the heart of the Teachings. *Maha Kundalini Shakti*, aka the Holy Spirit, shines through them as they go about their daily tasks, offering their blessing to each situation.

Faith is often confused with belief. Faith is complete trust (not blind acceptance)—the spiritual conviction which emerges from direct perception or direct experience. Faith is also the fruit of digested inner experience—the Holy Spirit working in us.

After we have received spiritual awakening, we begin to recognise within ourselves that there are many temporary states of consciousness. The Divine supra-causal or *turiya* state underpins them all and is present in all the other states whether we are aware of it or not. Yogic wakefulness means resting in the awareness of this most expanded state of consciousness, the seat of joy, bliss, unconditional love, and interconnectedness.

The spiritual practices of Sacred Feet Yoga, such as selfless service, hatha yoga, chanting, and meditation, develop this kind of wakefulness. When practiced faithfully, we are enabled to accept whatever is happening without getting hooked. We become absorbed into the whole experience without disengaging or analysing.

In this way, we become a pure, living offering and a radiant courier of the Holy Spirit.

St. Francis of Assisi, Somerset, KY. USA

SACRED FEET YOGA TEACHINGS
LEVEL TWO

The First Teachings
1. Practice self-inquiry
2. Expose your egoic projections.
3. Uproot your time-honored narratives.

The Second Teachings
1. Loosen your hold on lack.
2. Discern between love and need.
3. Let go of constriction and contrition.

The Third Teachings
1. Cooperate with purification.
2. Study the sacred energy commentaries.
3. Memorize the vibrations of sacred energy in your body.

The Fourth Teachings
1. Open to your deepest wisdom.
2. Place your greatness in the light.
3. Welcome your team of guides.

The Fifth Teachings
1. Focus on courage.
2. Partner with liberation, your own, other beings, the earth.
3. Be constant in your quest to live in an enlightened state.

Received by Swami Shraddhananda (aka Mataji) from her team of Siddha guides (May 5-7, 2017)

TEACHING 2.1.1

Practice self-inquiry.

On beginning the Second Level Teachings, we step into a deeper stage of *sadhana,* our spiritual journey.

When life seems difficult, every seeker would benefit from pausing and asking themselves, "What is in my mind, poison or honey? What comes up repeatedly in situations and people, where, and why? Are there events from earlier life/lifetimes that remind me of what I am feeling now? What buttons are being pushed and why? Am I these memories and thoughts?" In this way, we peel away the layers of the onion, arriving at the classical question, "Who am I?" Don't skip over these questions.

Ask the indwelling Holy Spirit, aka *Kundalini Shakti,* to reveal the triggers. From where do these awkward feelings and thoughts arise? Hold the question in meditation, as is shown in the practice below, and stay with each feeling in turn. Follow each one back to the source.

> Set a regular time aside to sit quietly. Allow the mind to soften its hold, and let the incoming and outflowing breath become your main focus for a few minutes, without changing it in any way. Lovingly ask the Holy Spirit to show you what needs to be known.

> Then, simply observe what is or is not happening, and follow your thoughts without judgement to their source. Should the mind remain busy, don't fight it. Simply ponder on the question, "Who am I?" Neither reject nor indulge in your thoughts. Observe as a witness, and let grace draw you inside.

> After completing the meditation, write about the experience. Journaling helps the reflection process and allows the deeper layers of the subconscious wisdom to surface.

This is the work of the spiritual path—to clear the veil of apparent separation and return to our natural, easy, happy state. The path of Divine knowledge begins by discerning for yourself the nature of your inner essence and then returning to and owning your own experience.

TEACHING 2.1.2

Expose your egoic projections.

Projection is one of Nature's oldest tricks. Our Consciousness is the screen upon which all the moods and perceptions are written. Most of this is unconscious until we reach a point in our *sadhana* (spiritual journey) when we receive *Shaktipat* (spiritual awakening). Then, we enter a whole different realm of inner experience. The individual soul is a reflection of pure Consciousness on the mind, and it is the reflection that gives rise to the sense of duality and differences.

When we practice self-inquiry, we begin to realise that how those perceptions dance on our screens is largely due to our past experiences and conditioning—our repeated tendencies (*samskaras*). We begin to perceive that what we see or feel in others arises from within our own minds.

The great enlightened Sages declare cryptically: "Thou Art That." This all-embracing experience of Divine vision is more comfortable to receive than to instill in our understanding. Why see the Divine in another? What is the effect on our minds? Recognising the dance of our mind superimposing itself on the "world" is a huge revelation for we realise that we can stop perpetuating the old tapes. We have the opportunity to reboot, reformulate, and transform our experience of life. We stop blaming others for our predicaments and states of mind, and those around us benefit, too, especially those close to us. At the most basic level, to experience joy and respect, we must offer joy and respect. When we offer anger or disgust to another, who will experience that?

Therefore, have a detached look at what quality of thoughts are coming up in the mind. Examine all the centuries-old baggage being carried within, respect the lessons it has brought you, and let it go. Weed out the poison and be persistent in cultivating good inner company.

TEACHING 2.1.3

Uproot your time-honored narratives.

What do we predominantly identify with—the light of Consciousness or its dance of names and forms? What lies at the root of your current experience? What memories are currently being triggered?

A field of golden buttercups looks very pretty in the sunshine. However, they present a challenge in a flowerbed for gardeners. The roots are tangled, and clever runners lie deep in the soil, sending out new shoots in every direction. Even when uprooted, little remnants remain in the soil ready to regenerate into new plants. The inner work is like this: one has to understand the nature of the mind's content and sift the soil carefully. And yet, buttercups in the right place are joyful expression of nature. We simply have to understand their exuberant attributes.

The stories we tell ourselves are like this. One small triggering incident may become the greatest drama after the memory retells it a few times, embellished with recollections from similar occurrences from the past. Then we become identified with the fiction created instead of the pure, unadulterated ground of being which is our real golden nature. The fictions we create about ourselves and others become part of our tangled personalities, and our sufferings are perpetuated.

Learn to identify the repetitive narratives and to resolve them in hand, one at a time. Keep a journal, and reflect on your triggering incidents and your hero/anti-hero themes. Notice how the mind glorifies the false narrative and wants to justify its actions. How long will we hold onto our treasured self-deceptions? Which narratives are your favourite themes? Untether yourself, and become free.

Ganesh (Ruler and Remover of Obstacles), Mornington Peninsula, Australia

TEACHING 2.2.1

Loosen your hold on lack.

Can you place your faith in the Divine Intelligence within yourself that knows your needs and supplies them in the fullness of time? This kind of trust loosens the fear that accompanies the sense of lack.

What is lack? It is the sense of not having enough. The sense of lack often places a person firmly in misery, in the corner of victimhood and fear, shutting the spirit down and closing it to the wealth that is present within and around a person. If ingrained, the sense of lack is often rooted in inherited family attitudes that run through generations of experiences. By breaking the spell of lack, we also set future generations free.

For abundance to flow, there must be the joy and freedom of spirit to be able to recognise it where it is present, fuelled by the sense of worthiness and an openness for acceptance.

Everyone has an abundance of something. Discover what you have in abundance by developing a gratitude list. This develops appreciation for what we do have. An antidote to the sense of lack is to give unconditionally with no expectation of reward.

Some do not realise how their kindness affects others, or how helpful their willingness to freely offer their time and listening skills is. What are your skills? How do you unconsciously express abundance? Loosen your hold on lack and appreciate your worth.

Offer your openness by giving. This openness enables us to let go of lack and fully receive. In the Bhagavad Gita, a much-revered scripture and guide for healthy spiritual life, Lord Krishna shows his love and appreciation for an open heart by accepting the sincere offering of even the smallest leaf.

AUTHOR'S CORRECTION

Page 21 The last paragraph should read:

'Give by offering your openness.'

TEACHING 2.2.2

Discern between love and need.

Do we know the difference between love and need? The two are often confused! The ability to discern means to distinguish, to separate, to sift. Discernment carries an element of detachment from personal bias and the perception of clear truth.

This ability to discern occurs from a very early age and is an essential skill to obtain what one needs for survival. A young child will try to work out what is needed, how to get it, and why one does not get it. In addition, wants and needs are often confused with emotions and reactions from not getting what one wants or needs immediately. A loving parent may be perceived as one who has a duty to provide a need.

Our storylines are set out in early infancy, and attitudes often require identifying and untangling before we realise that need is not necessarily the same as want, and that neither are the same as offering and being offered unconditional love. In addition, there are received cultural and religious ideas to consider.

Therefore, we would do well to recognise and understand what our basic needs are and to try to ensure that they are met, as well as to learn to distinguish between what is a healthy need and what is a misplaced neediness or dependence on another for fulfilment. This is a challenge when our old scripts and stories get in the way of healing and aligning with Spirit. We have to develop the capacity to honestly look at the deceptions we carry and to let them go before we can remain in the awareness of pure love.

This is where *Satsang* is invaluable—keeping the company of the Truth—that is, the company of those who hold the vibration of the Self and can fine tune us again and again, until we can consciously discern and hold the note for ourselves.

Madonna and Child, Chalice Gardens, Glastonbury, UK

TEACHING 2.2.3

Let go of constriction and contrition.

Constriction of consciousness is a natural phenomenon connected with human survival and the infant's development of name, form, and ego. As a child develops, the natural expanded state of infancy is caught up in the fascination of the world. Eventually, the soul forgets their divine experience, gets tangled up in the thrill of doer-ship, and rests in contraction. Like the parrot trained to perch on a pole, even after the chains have been taken away, the soul remains locked in its old stories and habits, bound to its limited viewpoint even though it is free to soar in awareness. As one poet declared, "Oh parrot on a pole, who has caught you?"

Contrition is an ego state that is often confused with remorse. It is essentially an act of smallness, a constriction of consciousness where the soul remains bound, born from a lack of faith in its own goodness. For some, contrition is an entrenched habit, a coping mechanism for handling circumstances that are out of control. It can hold us in a loop where we repeat the same behaviour over and over again.

Where there is remorse, one strives to reboot, whereas repeating "I'm sorry" as an unconscious habit merely entrenches the contracted state. A person who is "sorry" remains in a "sorry" state. An act of remorse, on the other hand, is an instance of restitution which opens the heart, a shift towards self-restoration and wholeness. There is insight propelled by grace which cultivates self-esteem, self-worth, and self-regard, all qualities that arise in the pure heart.

Practice: Follow the breath as constriction arises. Observe the behaviour pattern that arises, and follow it back to its source. Rest in the purity of your heart.

TEACHING 2.3.1

Cooperate with purification.

One of our key assets for co-operation with purification is enthusiasm. When we enter the spiritual arena and begin to tackle the veils that obscure our experience of light, we can feel despondent and overwhelmed. Furthermore, we think that "we" as the doer must orchestrate the clear-up.

However, the indwelling Holy Spirit is supremely intelligent. She automatically draws us to the right situations and people through which self-discovery and learning takes place. She is the indwelling grace that cleans up our inner subtle software, dislodging and flushing out those memories and tendencies that are held in the most subtle layer, the causal body that carries the deepest patterns from one incarnation to another.

The ego is intent on self-preservation. We can resist and make the ride harder for ourselves, or we can practice detachment and ease through whatever needs to be faced and released. Once this process is activated, many subtle experiences will surface. Some of them may be felt in meditation as fleeting sensations (known as cleansing actions or *kriyas*). Sensations such as heat or cold, body movements, flashes of insight, sound, colour, and pictures of scenes from the past may arise. Intense bliss or peace may course through the body and/or rise up through the central channel to the crown of our head.

Participate in one or more spiritual practices such as mantra repetition, chanting, and meditation to assist the process to run more smoothly. Engaging fully in daily life as *seva,* selfless service, is also a wonderful spiritual practice.

When the opportunity arises, consider taking the help of a seasoned Teacher to challenge the ego and to show you where you are caught.

TEACHING 2.3.2

Study the sacred energy commentaries.

As individuals, the journey to full self-recognition is unique to us. Each of us has to make our own discoveries, discharge our own misperceptions, and release what no longer serves us. However, there are signposts and experiences as well as pitfalls that are common factors for all seekers. When starting out, the kinds of experiences one might encounter can differ widely. Without a framework to aid understanding, they can be alarming and confusing; therefore, others' accurate insights are invaluable and dissipate fear as well as offer encouragement.

The sacred energy commentaries are written with great care and carry the deepest wisdom. In the past, they were guarded as secret treasures only available to the chosen few and were often coded to prevent misunderstanding. Usually, those given access to them were tutored by those who understood them. These days, we have access not only to many ancient commentaries such as the teachings of the Upanishads, the Bhagavad Gita, and the wealth of sacred texts from all the major traditions, but also to the spiritual biographies and talks of modern Shaktipat Gurus who have generously offered their wisdom. Today, we have excellent scholars who not only study the ancient sacred energy commentaries academically but also practice them experientially. In many cases, these texts are also an energetic transmission from the Teachers who gave them, which will serve to fuel your journey and activate it further. Many of these commentaries have been published or are accessible via the internet.

At Sacred Feet Yoga, our Teachers encourage students to study the sacred energy commentaries alongside their practices so that they may live in the experience of wisdom for themselves.

TEACHING 2.3.3

Memorize the vibrations of sacred energy in the body.

There are two aspects to the Holy Spirit—the cosmic and the internal. The Holy Spirit may pour in through the crown of our head and awaken deep insight and connection with everything. At the same time, its inner aspect lies within the body, dormant until activation.

The body is the doorway through which the Holy Spirit is awakened and experienced. Once the soul is mature enough, it begins to course through the physical and subtle bodies. The Holy Spirit, aka *Maha Kundalini Shakti*, may be perceived as a cleansing vibration which scours and fine tunes us, enabling us to fully shine. This flow is felt in many different ways, working through our body and our senses as well as being experienced in more subtle states. By recalling our own inner map of awareness, our memories serve as triggers to draw us back into the awareness of the Divine stream, the "Kingdom of Heaven," a state that we can return to again and again, entering the abode of Beingness joyfully and consciously.

Practice: Recall an instance of pure awareness. This could be a moment of blissful absorption in meditation, an "aha" moment whilst walking in nature, or rapture whilst listening to music. Notice how the whole being is engaged—body, mind, and spirit. Use the memory to transport your awareness into reconnection again, and bathe in the present moment. Allow yourself to dissolve the experiencer and become the fabric of the Universe experiencing.

Heart of a Tulip, Private Garden, England, UK

TEACHING 2.4.1

Open to your deepest wisdom.

The door opens with *Shaktipat*, the bestowal of grace that gives the inner awakening. Like a child, we are full of wonder at the access to our inner panorama. Many times, we return again and again through meditation, and yet, the inner scene is never quite the same. It is ever new, throwing up the delight of the Self alongside that which obscures it.

Once we start to examine and release our faulty programming, we may get disheartened. Progress may seem very slow; we might feel we are stuck on the shoreline instead of tasting the depths. Often, we are actually preparing to dive deeper by establishing good, firm foundations with our practices.

There is one really beneficial protocol we can follow when starting out, or when facing the next stage on a difficult journey, and that is to ask for help and protection from unnecessary diversions or mistakes.

Almost every spiritual undertaking begins with an invocation to the Divine, to either an externally conceived Deity or an internally perceived, deeper aspect of ourselves. This may be an elaborate ritual or traditional prayer empowered by centuries of use. Alternatively, a simple, respectful, sincere request may be the most appealing and effective method for you. An invocation basically calls forth grace, the operating energetic aspect of the Holy Spirit. Like the cry "All on board!" is made to signify the departure of a train, an invocation is a signal to the Self to dive deeper within and to open to our deepest wisdom, drawing our focus beyond the realms of names, forms, and mental concepts into the mystic oneness, joy, and peace that is always present, woven like threads into the fabric of our universe. When we actively open to receive, grace lovingly responds.

TEACHING 2.4.2

Place your greatness in the light.

Do we experience our greatness? Or do we experience our limitations? The vibratory energy which eventually manifests as thoughts, words, actions, and objects has the power to direct and misdirect our minds in untold ways. The playful Divine Consciousness enables and allows the sense of limitation to hold sway over us until we reach a certain point in our karma.

When the compassion of the Divine opens our awareness again to that greatness within, we yearn to recapture the glimpses of our own essential essence. It helps us to engage with sacred Teachings and to spend some quality time in the company of the wise. Doing so, we begin to resonate with their experience, and we rediscover our own greatness.

An enlightened Teacher has recognised their essential nature and anchored their awareness there. Greatness is no longer lost in the limitations of the ego. Since we are still learning to accept the experience of our Divine essence as our own, an enlightened Teacher may graciously remind us by imparting the experience of greatness and light repeatedly, until we are able to override the aeons of cultural, religious, and personal imprinting. Such Teachers model the original blueprint and hold it before us.

It takes time and determined willingness, along with a lot of grace, to uproot the repetitive language of limitation that we unwittingly impose on ourselves and accept from others. Thus, to enable our greatness to shine fully through everything we do, it is essential to reflect on where we do, and where we do not, own that greatness. Our sense of smallness serves no purpose, whereas the recognition of the inner light serves everyone.

Therefore, relinquish the yoke of limitation-consciousness.

TEACHING 2.4.3

Welcome your team of guides.

Countless enlightened Sages across the ages have declared: "Is there anywhere where the Divine is absent?"

Whilst this is true, each of us receives constant guidance from myriad sources for determining our decisions. Since many directions unconsciously derive from an accumulation of repeated habits and experiences both from ourselves and others, we need to develop discernment when making helpful and healthy decisions. This means exercising our listening skills deeply and widely beyond our usual boundaries of perception, learning to be open with our whole being.

There are archetypal energies that coalesce in Consciousness into Divine forms, that carry the wisdom and intelligence that is part of ourselves but is often hidden from full view.

We may perceive these as our "team of guides" or as "we" or perhaps as the gentle whisper within that resonates with Truth. Consciousness best communicates with itself through the more predominant of our subtle senses, so how that wisdom expresses can differ, sometimes emerging through images or hearing and other times through full blown interdimensional knowing. It takes patience to develop the Divine dialogue and to dive beneath the usual subconscious voices of the ego.

Meditation will help to develop that connection into the core of our being where our most reliable, still guides are also anchored. Journaling is also an effective method for learning to bypass the loud voices of the ego. Over time, the boundaries between the different layers of consciousness merge into the non-dual state of awareness, and then, wisdom is constantly and effortlessly expressed through us.

Meditating Buddha, Somerset, KY, USA

TEACHING 2.5.1

Focus on courage.

We do need courage when dealing with ordinary decisions and situations in life and even more so when walking the spiritual path. Courage is necessary when riding the rapids of a fast river, as we don't know when we will merge with the sweet stillness and stability of the ocean. Sometimes, we might want to rest in the safety of what is known.

Nevertheless, the Holy Spirit encourages us to move forward as we face uncomfortable aspects of ourselves, the places where we are stuck. Sometimes, that means we must let go of our cherished ideas, step forward into the unknown, and allow life to teach us new ways of being and experiencing. For many of us, courage is a quality we don't think we have.

Actually, whilst we can ask for help and invoke courage, the helpful qualities we are seeking are ready to support us from within. All that is needed is conscious connection with the Holy Spirit. Then we hold our seats, holding the reins of the chariot, trusting that we can shine by giving Her space to work through us. In this way, even when we don't feel courageous, courage will rise up in abundance to support us!

In a retreat on the theme of courage, Swami Shraddhananda, Founder of Sacred Feet Yoga, emphasized the importance of courage on the spiritual path with these powerful words:

"Have the courage to take your seat in meditation. Have the courage to practice self-inquiry. Have the courage to move out of poverty consciousness. Have the courage to loosen your hold on lack. Have the courage to co-operate with purification. Have the courage to be a Guru, one who leads people out of darkness into light. Have the courage to attain the consciousness of the Guru. Claim your Dharma."

TEACHING 2.5.2

Partner with liberation, your own, other beings, the earth.

As our discernment is refined, the Holy Spirit reveals the inner treasures of the universe. She shows us glimpses of the awesome, scintillating light that pervades everything, from the paving stones in the streets to the trees that shelter us, the people passing by, and even the particles sparkling in the air we breathe. We begin to recognise the fabric of Supreme Consciousness that runs like a golden thread throughout the universe of names and forms. Our vision and understanding become re-oriented. The subtle senses are purified and harnessed, and the will of the individual becomes available as a cleansed instrument in service to the universal will. The dissected world of "me versus them" shifts into the world of "we." Experiencing the bliss of One-ness, we relinquish our identification with contracted states and glamours such as power, self-indulgence, and acquisition. Instead, we anchor into the liberated state.

By partnering with liberation, we live a life where our actions and our thinking reflect and fully embrace inclusivity and One-ness. Consciousness, whilst supremely free, partners with us on every level, and we, in turn, offer our support and engagement with other beings, nature, and Mother Earth herself.

When any part of Her seems unbalanced or damaged, we feel it and can offer restoration in practical ways. We can do this by offering our regular spiritual practices to hold the vibration of peace and joy, allowing the healing vibrations to radiate out into the world. We can uplift others individually by offering that light to them. We can practice sacred activism to protect and uplift the environment. Explore and enable your own contribution to emerge from within.

Woodpecker Feather Resting on Calcite, England, UK

TEACHING 2.5.3

Be constant in your quest to live in an enlightened state.

Each one of us unfolds in our own way. As we mature, we may find that the practices that originally kindled our path may be supplanted by others such as meditation and *seva* (selfless service). Sometimes, we stay with a practice, or we may return to earlier practices with deeper understanding.

We may also face common stumbling blocks or become out of balance with the rest of life—and may need to check in with our inner guidance to modify our approach. At each stage, we need to take a detached look at what is happening, adjust, and keep the fire nourished. Increasingly, we realise that the real work being undertaken is to merge, to become fully established in the awareness and joy of Supreme Consciousness all the time, in every breath and heartbeat, until our awareness becomes one long, seamless moment. We draw from what we have learned in our formal practices and apply the wisdom in the here and now. Initially, attention oscillates; the long gaps between spans of attention become shorter with practice.

Identify the triggers that draw your attention outwards and make you drop awareness. Reset your intention every day to practice consciously, and ask for grace and perseverance.

Then, practice maintaining full attention whilst going about daily tasks. Without changing the flow, observe the breath as it moves in and out of the body. Experiment and discover how you can stay constant, connected, and fully present—using whatever works for you.

Above all, know that you are loved, blessed, and supported by the grace of the Holy Spirit together with the whole community of holy beings who live in an enlightened state.

SACRED FEET YOGA TEACHINGS
LEVEL THREE

The First Teachings
1. Sacred is everywhere.
2. Discern the path to your sacred feet.
3. Grace does not make mistakes.

The Second Teachings
1. Abide in the breath.
2. Abide in your own deep heart.
3. Abide in the nectar of *purno'ham*, completeness.

The Third Teachings
1. Let go of ego's concerns.
2. Release all expectations.
3. Dissolve the fear of separation.

The Fourth Teachings
1. Reboot in every moment.
2. Listen with attention.
3. Be happy; revel in the joy of being.

The Fifth Teachings
1. Recognize the Divine Essence in all.
2. Serve unconditionally. Love all, reject none.
3. Merge in the heart of the universe.

Received by Swami Prakashananda from her team of Siddha guides, at the time of Swami Shraddhananda's Transition (February 16, 2021)

TEACHING 3.1.1

Sacred is everywhere.

This Teaching encapsulates the heart of all the other Teachings. It is a handle to freedom. If you can penetrate the depths of this teaching, you will realise the essence of all experience.

Sacred has been defined as that which is holy, the transcendent state expressing the core of existence and ultimate being. In reality, this essence, this sacredness, is all pervasive. "The Sacred," aka Absolute Consciousness, is the real Self. The Sacred doesn't just run like a river of gold through everything we do and are, it IS the river of gold itself unfolding upon our screens of awareness, expressing as myriad forms and names, and what we identify as "we," are part of the play. This is not just a concept but is an expression of direct experience and the fruit of Yoga. Indeed, there is a well-known aphorism from the *Svacchandra-tantra* which attests to this. It states, "*Nashivam Vidyate Kvachit*," which loosely translated means, "There is nowhere where God is not."

Little children do experience this as their natural state. They take delight in every mundane encounter and discovery, considering each moment as magical. With open hearts and little or no conditioning to obstruct their experience, a young child's wonder is obvious. Their sacred appreciation and participation is an unconscious one. Here is a simple practice for cultivating this awareness:

> Set aside some time for a walk. Bring your attention to the breath, simply observing without changing the rhythm.
>
> As you walk, maintain a wide-eyed focus, looking out from the back of your head to encompass the whole sweep of vision. At the same time, take in all the sensory experience, such as the sounds and colours around you, without identifying or rejecting anything.
>
> You may find that the mind chatter kicks in, or that your focus contracts and is drawn to something in particular, but as with the other stimuli, neither reject nor engage. Simply allow "YOU" to fall away.
>
> Embrace the Self and anchor there.

TEACHING 3.1.2

Discern the path to your sacred feet.

Many traditions have honored the feet of the Holy Ones. Most Westerners will be familiar with the time when the Master Jesus, with great humility, washed the feet of his disciples, a moment that truly shocked them. Not only was he ritually removing their faulty thinking and subtle debris, but he also was showing them that they were equal and perfectly worthy of experiencing the state of Oneness.

Some will be aware that the energies of awakened beings flow out abundantly from their feet. For this reason, devotees will respectfully touch the feet of saints to receive blessings, and the sandals of such saints are often placed on altars, understanding that the blessings emanating from them will uplift all those around.

On a deeper level, the sacred feet represent spiritual balance, inner absorption, and, ultimately, complete union with the Divine, the highest spiritual realization. The two feet express the statement "Thou art That," where the Divine Self and the inner Self are realized as the profound union of the two. They also represent the mantra *Hamsa*, the natural sound of the inbreath and outbreath, the balancing of *prana*.

The path to your sacred feet is a journey of perception and understanding. William Blake once said, "If the doors of perception were cleansed everything would appear to man as it is, Infinite." This awakened path guided by the Holy Spirit takes us from duality to non-duality awareness. We learn to embody the wisdom of the inner Teacher and to anchor it into our everyday world of action.

First, we climb the "mountain" of spiritual practices and experience the inner fire of *Kundalini Shakti* that dissolves and flushes away the debris of past traumas and experiences held in our subtle bodies. Then, we bring the fruits of our journey back down into the world as an offering for all, who are now no longer perceived as the "other" but recognised as an expression of the same one divine consciousness. In this way, water is veritably changed into wine.

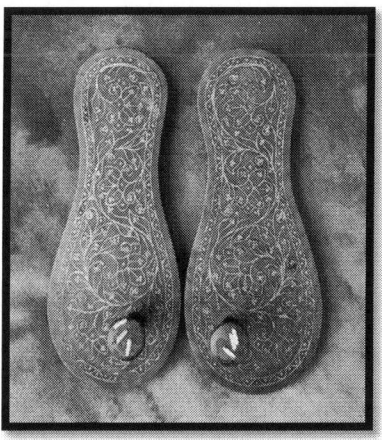

Padukas (Sacred Sandals)
Sw. Prakashananda's Private Puja, Letchworth, UK

TEACHING 3.1.3

Grace does not make mistakes.

What is grace? How shall we understand it? A great modern spiritual Master recently proclaimed: "Grace is God's *prasad*." In India, *prasad* is an unconditional, free offering bestowed after a visit to a holy place or being. *Prasad* traditionally takes the form of food or flowers, although it can take any form, and is infused with the energetic blessings of the Divine.

Grace flows abundantly but it is also true that some self-effort is involved, in that one must be open to receiving it and able to recognize grace for what it is. So often we ask internally for some change in our circumstances or for a greater depth of understanding and connection, for integration, but when change presents itself in a way that seems contrary to our expectations, we dismiss it, or even fight against it, seeing it as misfortune. Yet, it is we ourselves who have opened ourselves up to grace, and we who hold expectations about what form it should take.

Understand that grace is the action of the Divine flowing through us, and that grace carries all the Divine qualities, being all knowing, all pervasive, and supremely intelligent. "That" within us knows what is needed. Our current circumstances give us the perfect prescription, the forum through which we can learn and grow.

Grace does not make mistakes.

Have the courage to welcome grace, whatever form it takes. Before each action, invoke grace. Let it surge up within you, and have gratitude for everything that happens.

Finally, whatever is presenting itself to you on your spiritual path, there is a simple practice that bears tremendous fruit: See everything as *Prasad*.

TEACHING 3.2.1

Abide in the breath.

One of the easiest ways to abide in the breath is to meditate on *Hamsa*, meaning "I am That." This can be done wherever you are, whatever you are doing, since the breath is always with you. "Ham" and "Sa" represent the natural sounds of the breath through inhalation and exhalation, and the individual soul. At a more expanded level, these are the natural sounds of the Self, the inner breath of awareness, the undivided Consciousness that is Self-existent and immortal.

Start by sitting in a quiet spot where the back can be comfortably straight. Take one or two deep breaths, relaxing and releasing any obvious tension in the body. Now bring your attention to the rhythm of the breath itself as it moves in and out, allowing the breath to settle naturally, without forcing it in any way. Become aware of the natural sound "Ham" as the breath enters into the body and the sound "Sa" as it flows out. Follow the in breath into the inner space of your being and the out breath as it flows into the outer space outside.

Simply observe and allow any unbidden thoughts to fall away. If you find you have picked up and followed a particular thread of thought, which is very normal, especially when first taking up meditation, simply and gently bring your awareness back to the breath again. After a while, as your body relaxes more deeply, you may find that the breath may get smaller or seem to disappear completely. Don't worry if this happens. It is perfectly normal in deep relaxation for this to happen (and the Divine intelligence within you will deepen the breath automatically when you need it).

Sometimes, *Hamsa* reverses into *So'ham*. Sometimes, other phenomena may arise. That's fine. Simply trust that the Divine inner intelligence knows exactly what you need in this moment. Rest in the sweet stillness of your own Divine nature. When it's time to come out of meditation, take a few deep, long breaths, slowly and mindfully bringing your awareness back into the room again.

This is a very effective and deeply nourishing practice, and you might not realise just how deeply relaxed you have become, so make sure that you are fully grounded before resuming everyday activities like driving. You may find it helpful to eat something sweet or to drink a glass of water to bring your awareness fully back to everyday activities again.

TEACHING 3.2.2

Abide in your own deep heart.

The heart referred to here is something deeper than sentiment and more expansive than the physical heart. The Teaching is alluding to the centre point of our entire being, the hub from which all activity arises. The ancients encourage us to enter the *madhya*, our own deep heart, the inner expression of our essential essence that lies at the root of our being. Sometimes, they refer to entering the "cave of the heart," the resting place where the mind and heart are unified.

Whilst we may initially experience this abiding in the heart as a meditation state that we leave and return to, it is, in reality, our natural default state. We can train ourselves to reclaim that original awareness and keep our attention there, in the place within us that is steady and unchanging.

On the spiritual path, we develop the qualities of steadiness and resilience. We learn to "hold our seat," not just in meditation, but through all the circumstances of our lives, both smooth and rough. Like Arjuna in the *Bhagavad Gita*, keeping his balance in the chariot, we hold the reins, the forces of life, whilst relinquishing the limited perceptions of ego and allowing Krishna, who represents his inner Teacher, the Divine wisdom within him, to lead the direction. It takes both courage and persistent practice to ride through the rough patches of life whilst maintaining the awareness of those around us. The path of the heart is not just a meditation practice but is the full offering of our whole being to whatever life is presenting.

Whenever you feel shut down or deflated, remember, the solution is only a heartbeat away, as close as your breath. This is the time to engage with practical, grounding tasks, activities that engage the body. This is why the practice of *seva*, selfless service, is so beneficial. The ego and the chattering mind step aside, the wanting "me" and sense of "otherness" disappear, and we quite naturally enter into the stream of life itself, into the expansion of the universal heart.

Heart of a Rose, Private Garden, England, UK

TEACHING 3.2.3

Abide in the nectar of *purno'ham*, completeness.

A disciple once asked the great saint Shankaracharya, "Who is God?" He replied, "The witness of your mind." A ripe disciple will receive that reply as a direct transmission of the enlightened state and fall open completely. For most, it takes a little longer. We may need to undergo some purification, a cleaning of our spectacles!

The *Ashtavakra Gita* states: "If you witness your body distinctively and abide, relaxing in awareness itself, then immediately you will be joyful, peaceful and free from blockages" (1.4). There is always a part of us, the witness, that is awake. Even when our attention is absorbed elsewhere, when someone shouts fire, we are immediately alert. Consciousness continues its play through each individual whether we are awake to it or not.

Our egos may ignore this message for a while, or only understand with the mind, but its meaning slowly sinks in, nevertheless. Like a bee to nectar, we are inexorably drawn. When we finally recognise it with our whole being, we exclaim, "Oh yes, of course!" The vibration and joy inherent in the declaration of *purno'ham* (meaning "I am perfect. I am the all-pervasive, universal fullness itself. I am complete.") arises from recognition of the Divine within us, our essential nature. Even one glimpse will continue to unfold subtly within the consciousness of the recipient. Once recognised, the wise remain anchored in the state of *purno'ham*. One realises that there is nowhere to go and nothing to be attained.

Pause for a moment. Widen your focus to take in everything within and around you. Can you recognise your completeness? Without assessing or analysing what arises within, without letting your focus be drawn to any detail, simply savour the perfect stillness and tranquillity of the ocean of awareness. The nectar of *purno'ham* is all-pervasive and totally complete, and like the flute through which music is played, those who are free do not hold onto the notes being played through them.

Abide then in your own fullness, which is perfect, complete, and unaffected by any modification of the mind.

TEACHING 3.3.1

Let go of ego's concerns.

Does ego really exist? Let us consider… Each spark of consciousness collects its own identifiable markers, a jumble of memories, habits, and associations that assume importance in our minds. The tendency for identification with the body further limits our experience and emphasizes the sense of individuality and separation consciousness. This activity is labelled as ego, and although there is an assumption of form, it is really a convenient handle to describe an aspect of the phenomena of contraction.

In the physical world, we have learned to use the "ego" to escalate our own intentions. The ego's tendency is for posturing, for being the central hero on every stage. Sadly, we get lost in the play and lose the fullness and effectiveness of all the Divine properties as they play through us. Let go of ego's concerns. Concerns take us away from the full experience of the Divine.

Bhagavan Nityananda, one of the 20th century's greatest self-realized masters taught: "One must seek the shortest way and the fastest means to get back home—to turn the spark within into a blaze, to be merged in and to identify with that greater fire which ignited the spark."

Reflect. What are your preoccupations right now? Do they create the sense of separation or expansion of awareness? Who is in charge?

The Master Jesus taught his students to consider shifting perspective to one of expansive inclusion in the Lord's prayer. The words are so familiar to us that the message is mostly lost. Consider the deeper meaning of this intention: "Thy will be done on Earth, as it is in Heaven."

In the *Bhagavad Gita*, where the whole spiritual journey is depicted, Arjuna's sense of separation finally dissolves, and full realization emerges. He finally relinquishes his role as hero and surrenders, with the simple statement, "I will do thy bidding."

Surrender your preoccupations, and rest in your full, joyful, luminous Self.

TEACHING 3.3.2

Release all expectations.

A lot of "helpful" advice is offered out these days on how to manifest your goals, under the guise of spirituality. Mostly, these objectives are an extension of the ego on a subtle level. Ask who is it that wants something to turn out a certain way?

This kind of thinking arises when Consciousness limits itself. As the nondual teachings of the *Shiva Sutras* attest, "Limited knowledge is bondage" (1.2). When identification with the totality of the Self is restricted, the constricting veils kick in, and the mind relies on limited data received through the gross and subtle senses.

Nevertheless, whilst we embrace the physical world and its needs, we can still live in an expanded state, without attachment to outcomes. With understanding, we can set our goals without holding onto egoic expectations. Do "we" know what is needed, or is it our wants that are being addressed?

Know that each time we have expectations attached to our goals and actions, we have been hooked by the ego and have limited the possibilities. When we let go of our expectations, we allow the divine creative flow to offer wonderful outcomes that is not confined to our limited vision of how things should be. Try this practice to release expectations:

> Have a pencil and paper at hand. Just for a moment, close your eyes, relax your focus on outside stimuli, and allow the pencil to draw unguided across the page. Let Consciousness lead and draw freely without the interference of the mind.

> Now, open your eyes and take your pencil again. Write. Or draw, if that helps you to express better. Simply allow Consciousness to move through you, without predetermining what might be articulated. There is an exhilarated freedom when no outcome is projected and the potential of the new is enabled.

> Release all expectations and allow Consciousness to take the reins of your chariot.

TEACHING 3.3.3

Dissolve the fear of separation.

Mature meditators experience that we manifest both as the world and as universal Consciousness. As the world, the sense of individuality produces the phenomena of birth and death. We appear to be separate from others but, in reality, there is no actual separation (and no real birth or death either). There is only the dance of Universal Consciousness, ever expanding and contracting.

Sages have documented the preliminary subtle stages of separation that occur when Universal Consciousness chooses to restrict itself. The unlimited qualities such as self-revelation, absolute bliss, divine will, omniscience, and the ability to assume any form are masked by the obscuring forces that create the sense of differentiation.

In the world, the first apparent separation takes place with the physical detachment from the Mother at birth, although the bonding does not fully disconnect for a few years. Fear arises... Without the spiritual awakening that occurs when the Holy Spirit, aka *Maha Kundalini Shakti*, is activated, the individual spark operating in the world of names and forms only has limited access to its own magnificence.

At the point of death, whether temporarily through disassociation or by dropping the body altogether, one comes to understand that there is no such thing as death, and our fear dissolves as we touch our essential essence.

In meditation, we learn to consciously recognise the deepest part of ourselves, the unchanging inner centre that we can return to again and again. Fear disappears automatically when that inner core of being is experienced. Every meditation can be considered as a "mini death" where our attachment to the gross and subtle elements, the mind, and the intellect is allowed the fall away. The Holy Spirit, aka *Maha Kundalini Shakti*, melts away the impediments, the faulty vision that prevents us from seeing clearly.

Yogis practice *Yoga Nidra*, where the gradual withdrawal of the body, senses, and mind (*pratyahara*) is consciously practiced in a series of steps. This tapping into the state of relaxed alertness is the preliminary stage that enables one to experience full immersion in the bliss of the inner self. Practice maintaining that state as the world manifests again.

Abhaya Mudra (Gesture of Fearlessness, Protection, and Peace)
Shiva Nataraj, Anugraha House, Somerset, KY, USA

TEACHING 3.4.1.

Reboot in every moment.

There are occasions that require our minds to intentionally focus on specific tasks, where our attention helps us to operate in the world of names and forms. However, much of our time and energy is dissipated. When we take up the discipline of inner silence, then whatever we undertake naturally becomes sharp and productive.

Reboot in every moment. Refresh the inner screen. Every single time you become aware of dropping into the inner chatter of the mind, every time your focus is unconsciously drawn outside, bring your attention back into the present moment.

Sitting formally for contemplative prayer, meditation, and other practices that still the mind are very useful when practiced regularly. It is recommended that you reinforce your practice where possible by setting aside a special time and place where the vibrations can build up and support you, much in the same way that churches and temples that are regularly prayed in have an environment of peace and stillness. Ideally, your practice will extend beyond your formal time into the whole day even whilst moving around your daily activities.

There are various methods for educating the mind to keep the attention in the present. Mantra repetition—*Om Namah Shivaya*, *Om Mani Padme Hum*, the Jesus prayer and *Hamsa* awareness, following the breath, are some common examples. When enlivened, the vibration of the mantras will help to disperse the veils and call forth the clarity of the Self.

Muslims bring the awareness of the Divine into their daily activities by setting aside five dedicated times a day, and often more, praying the *Salah*, an embodied prayer infused with peace and divine blessing.

The Sacred Feet Hatha Yoga sequences taught by the Sacred Feet Yoga Senior Acharyas are another empowered embodiment of the Teachings, as is the practice of Sacred Feet Reiki.

Sooner or later, the discipline of attention will bear fruit.

TEACHING 3.4.2

Listen with attention.

God speaks in the silence of the heart. Listening is the beginning of prayer.
— Mother Teresa

Listen with full attention, with your whole being. The universe is a seamless whole, excluding nothing. When artists paint, they don't just look at the objects, they pay attention to the whole subject matter, including all the shapes and spaces between the objects. A tree does not grow in a vacuum, but in relationship to the earth and sky around it. In the same way, we need to use our whole awareness and not simply our ears.

When we first start listening with attention, we discover that most noise in our minds is generated by ourselves. Most of the content is a salad of random thoughts, a jumping from one memory association to another. It is not coherent, being mostly self-centred day dreaming, where we are the hero/ine, a celebration of the ego. How often is a conversation an opportunity to advance our own opinions rather than an opportunity to learn and a genuine, respectful offering of our time to others? Furthermore, what we hear is mostly interpretation of what we receive from others since it is affected by our inner filters.

Practice listening without attaching commentary. Listen to the space between thoughts, the space between the exhalation and inhalation. Listen to the inner sounds that arise from deep sustained silence, the sounds of nature around us, and the input of wisdom from our inner guides.

This readiness to listen keenly with attention, without the input of the ego, without agendas, enables us to rest in the Self whilst functioning in the world. It enables us to receive the grace and wisdom of the Divine, and it enables us to function as a hollow bamboo where the Divine can offer love and light in the world without anything impeding its flow.

TEACHING 3.4.3

Be happy; revel in the joy of being.

People travel to wonder at the height of the mountains, at the huge waves of the seas, at the long course of the rivers, at the vast compass of the ocean, at the circular motion of the stars, and yet they pass by themselves without wondering. — St. Augustine

Who cannot be drawn by the laughter of young infants who dwell in the natural state of happiness? Their state is infectious, reminding us of our own hidden sweetness. Instantly, we set aside our current mood and resonate with their vibration.

If you don't feel happy right now, how can you recover? There is a whole palette of methods. Experiment and see what works best for you. Try journalling to let go of your current preoccupations, not to bypass them, but to release them from your mind. Then, find some activity that takes your focus away from yourself. Offer your time and attention to another, take a walk in the fresh air, or listen to your favourite restorative music. Sometimes, it is enough to reinforce a positive state by simply acting as if you are happy. As you think, so you become.

The pure, unadulterated joy of being arises from within you. It is your natural default state, your original blueprint. It isn't something that can be generated from an outside source. The ego thinks it is something that can be accessed by acquiring things or investing in temporary experiences and relationships. Of course, even when contracted, we certainly glimpse the inner vibration of joy reflected in otherness, since the outer world is a creative expression of joy and carries its signature.

Place some chocolate or ice cream in your mouth. Let it rest on the tongue and allow it to slowly melt. Receive the whole experience without doing anything, allowing it to transport your attention right back to the source, going deeper within, stripping away the sensory and mental layers of perception. Remain fully present.

Embrace the joy of being that sustains everything that you are.

Oceanside, Mornington Peninsula National Park, Australia

TEACHING 3.5.1.

Recognize the divine essence in all.

The *Shiva Sutras* say, "The Self is an actor" (3.9). One being, one Consciousness, expresses through multiple forms—the vibration is seeded in everything.

The Lord's Club story tells of a group of Lords who decided to form an exclusive club. This presented everyone with a problem. Since all were Lords, there were no servants to undertake the menial tasks. "Who will do the chores?" asked one Lord. "We all will," said another, "Let's all take turns!" And so they did, each week rotating the various roles. The Lord who mopped the floor one week would find himself cooking a banquet the next. The one selected to arrange the flowers would find himself fixing the plumbing the following week. The beauty of it was that they enjoyed every task because they never forgot that they were Lords! And even though each Lord was in disguise, they could still recognise the Lord in each other.

In the same way, actors on the stage know who they are. They don't forget their real identity when acting in a play. When we are conscious of our essential nature, neither do we. We simply play the game well and do it with enthusiasm and joy.

Welcome everyone with love and respect as your own Beloved. Even if you are shy or unconvinced, do it anyway.

By repeatedly calling forth the divine essence of the Self in others, one naturally resonates with all the myriad names and forms of Consciousness and begins to experience each one with great joy.

TEACHING 3.5.2

Serve unconditionally. Love all, reject none.

Recognising that we are all members of the Lord's Club who are playing different roles, we can no longer be fooled by the common deception of the majority. We know who we are, and we recognise ourselves in each other, much as bees recognise themselves to be part of the one hive.

Selfless service helps us to cultivate and maintain this awareness. It may be taken up as a specific practice where a task is undertaken regardless of skill set! On the other hand, this is an approach where every daily activity can be handled as selfless service. This practice is a wonderful opportunity to reflect on unconscious attitudes and judgements. We learn to consider and appreciate others without judging them. Just as we don't reject or conceive our fingers and toes to be other than our body, perception shifts to accept all as part of our own extended being. We learn to love all and reject none!

Whilst it is a natural trick of Consciousness to contract into individuality, once we have tasted wholeness even once, we are no longer fooled. The road to real inner freedom does not exclude others. It is inclusive. We may perceive so many ears and eyes, so many minds and hearts, a kaleidoscope of sensory and mental impressions; however, underneath it all, Consciousness expresses, "I am the One Light shining everywhere. Wherever you are, I am there. My Light and love is reflected in everything you perceive."

The Divine includes every experience. Embrace all beings as your Beloved. As the Master Jesus taught, "Love one another. As I have loved you, so you must love one another" (John 15:12).

As he so well knew, love is the easiest door and pathway into the awareness of the Divine. We in turn come to recognise that selfless love is the very essence, the very heart of everything.

Cross, Anugraha House, Somerset, KY

TEACHING 3.5.3

Merge in the heart of the universe.

Here is an early Christian prayer taught by St. Patrick to the Irish. It is a clear and simple practice that can be done whilst sitting formally or when walking around:

> Christ with me, Christ before me, Christ behind me, Christ in me, Christ beneath me, Christ above me, Christ on my right, Christ on my left, Christ when I lie down, Christ when I sit down, Christ in the heart of everyone who thinks of me, Christ in the mouth of everyone who speaks of me, Christ in the eye that sees me, Christ in the ear that hears me.

And here is a modified *Nyasa*, a powerful practice that amplifies the awareness of divinity in every part of your being:

> Begin your practice by bowing in all directions to the Divine as your most precious Beloved. Your Beloved may take a particular form such as Jesus, Shiva, the Goddess, your Guru, or your mantra. Mindfully invoke their presence and blessings.
>
> Move into a steady, seated posture, with the back comfortably straight. Settle into the breath for a few moments and then begin to install your preferred form of the Beloved in each part of you.
>
> Placing your hands on your head, say to yourself, "My Beloved is in my head." Infuse your words with great love and feeling. Slowly move down the body, placing your hands in turn, over your ears, then eyes, mouth, neck, shoulders, chest, heart, trunk, thighs, knees, calves, and feet, pausing each time to really invoke the presence of the Beloved in each part of you. Experience the energetic flow of grace pouring through you.
>
> Slowly reverse the process, moving from the feet through each part again until you reach your head. Repeat to yourself with firm conviction: "I am in my Beloved, and my Beloved is in me."

In this way, all sense of separation dissolves. There is no more inside or outside, there is only the pulsating heart of pure, radiant being. Experiencing everything as the Beloved, may you merge in the heart of the universe.

FURTHER READING

Adyashanti. Emptiness Dancing. Sounds True, Inc., 2006.

Sw. Anubhavananda. Fundamentals of Life (Based on Shiva Sutras). Sat Bhavana Trust, India, 2013.

Karen Armstrong. The Great Transformation: The Beginning of Our Religious Traditions. Anchor, 2007.

Douglas Baker and Celia Hansen. Super-Consciousness Through Meditation. Samuel Weiser, Inc., 1978.

The Bhagavad-Gita: Krishna's Counsel in Time of War. Barbara Stoller Miller, tr. Bantam Classics, 1986.

Cynthia Bourgeault. The Wisdom of Jesus: Transforming Heart and Mind—A New Perspective on Christ and His Message. Shambhala, 2008.

_____. The Wisdom Way of Knowing: Reclaiming an Ancient Tradition to Awaken the Heart. Jossey-Bass, 2003.

Malcolm Boyd. Are You Running with Me, Jesus? Cowley Publications, 2006. 40th Anniversary Edition.

Douglas Renfrew Brooks. Auspicious Wisdom. State University of New York Press, 1992.

_____. The Secret of The Three Cities: An Introduction to Hindu Sakta Tantrism. The University of Chicago Press, 1998.

Rainero Cantalamessa. Sober Intoxication of the Spirit: Filled with the Fullness of God. Servant Books, 2005.

Sw. Chidvilsananda (Gurumayi Chidvilasananda). Courage and Contentment. Introduction by Stratford Sherman. SYDA Foundation, 1999.

_____. Inner Treasures. Introduction by Constantina Rhodes Bailey. SYDA Foundation, 1995.

_____. The Yoga of Discipline. Introduction by David M. Katz. SYDA Foundation, 1996.

Kavitha Chinnaiyan, MD. Shakti Rising: Embracing Shadow and Light on the Goddess Path to Wholeness. Non-duality Press. 2021.

William Chittick. The Self-Disclosure of God: Principles of Ibn Al-Arabi's Cosmology. Suny Press, 1997.

Ani Pema Chodron. No Time to Lose: A Timely Guide to the Way of the Bodhisattva. Helen Berliner, ed. Shambhala, 2005.

Rabbi David A. Cooper. God Is a Verb: Kabbalah and the Practice of Mystical Judaism. Riverhead Books, 1998.

Gabriel Cousens. Spiritual Nutrition: Six Foundations for Spiritual Life and the Awakening of Kundalini. North Atlantic Books, 2005.

His Holiness the Dalai Lama XIV of Tibet. Comfort and Ease: The Vision of Enlightenment in the Great Perfection. Foreword by Sogyal Rinpoche. Wisdom Publications, 2007.

Sw. Durgananda. The Heart of Meditation. SYDA Foundation, 2002. Re-published as Meditation for the Love of It. Sally Kempton. Sounds True, Inc., 2010.

Mark S.G. Dyczkowski. The Doctrine of Vibration: An Analysis of the Doctrines and Practices of Kashmir Shaivism. State University of New York Press, 1987.

_____. Tantraloka: The Light on, and of the Tantras, Vols. 1-11. Amazon, 2023.

Georg Feuerstein. Tantra: The Path of Ecstasy. Shambhala, 1998.

Paul Fiddes. "The Theology of the Charismatic Movement." In Strange Gifts: A Guide to Charismatic Renewal. David Martin and Peter Mullen, eds. Blackwell, 1984.

Elizabeth Gilbert. Eat, Pray, Love. Penguin Books, 2006.

Philip Goldberg. American Veda. Foreword by Huston Smith. Harmony Books, 2010.

Thich Nhat Hanh. Living Buddha, Living Christ. Introduction by Elaine Pagels. Foreword by Brother David Stenindl-Rast. Riverhead Books, 2007.

_____. You Are Here: Discovering the Magic of the Present Moment. Shambhala, 2009.

Joan Shivarpita Harrigan. Kundalini Vidya: The Science of Spiritual Transformation. Patanjali Kundalini Yoga Care, Sixth Edition, 2005.

Andrew Harvey. The Direct Path. Broadway Books, 2000.

M.V. Hatengdi. Nityananda: The Divine Presence. Foreword by Sw. Chetanananda. Rudra Press, 1984.

Quincy Howe, Jr. Reincarnation for the Christian. The Theosophical Publishing House, 1987. First edition, Westminster Press, 1974.

J.J. Hurtak. "The Holy Spirit: The Feminine Aspect of the Godhead." The Academy for Future Science, 1993. http://www.adishakti.org

William James. The Varieties of Religious Experience. Classic Books International, 2010.

Kurt Johnson and David Robert Ord. The Coming Interspiritual Age. Namaste, 2012.

Sonya Jones aka Sw. Shraddhananda. Are You Dancing With Me Shiva? (poems). Sacred Feet Publishing Imprint.

_____. Jesus Was a Shaktipat Guru. Sacred Feet Publishing Imprint, 2014.

_____. Small Claims, Large Encounters (poems). Brito & Lair, 1995.

Sonya Jones aka Sw. Shraddhananda et al… Mature Interspirituality – Wayne Teasdale's Nine Elements and Beyond (compilation of essays by multiple authors). Sacred Feet Publishing Imprint, 2017.

Anodea Judith. Eastern Body, Western Mind: Psychology and the Chakra System as a Path to the Self. Celestial Arts, 2004.

_____. The Sevenfold Journey: Reclaiming Mind, Body and Spirit Through the Chakras. Crossing Press, 1993.

_____. Wheels of Life: A User's Guide to the Chakra System. Llewellyn Publications, 1987.

Fr. Thomas Keating. Open Mind, Open Heart. Continuum, 1986. Twentieth Anniversary Edition, 2006.

Sally Kempton. Awakening Shakti. Sounds True, Inc., 2013.

Sw. Kripananda. The Guru's Sandals: Threshold of the Formless. SYDA Foundation, 1997.

_____. The Sacred Power: A Seeker's Guide to Kundalini. SYDA Foundation, 1995.

Gopi Krishna. The Evolutionary Energy in Man. Shambhala, 1997. First published in Great Britain by Vincent Stuart & John M. Watkins, Ltd., 1970.

Zachary F. Lansdowne. The Chakras and Esoteric Healing. Motilal Banarsidass, 1993. First published by Samuel Weiser, 1986.

Sw. Lakshmanjoo and John Hughes. Shiva Sutras: The Supreme Awakening. Author House, 2007.

Sw. Lakshmanjoo. Vijnana Bhairava: The Practice of Centering Awareness. Indica Books, 2007.

C.W. Leadbeater. The Chakras. Quest Books, 1997. Copyright 1927 by The Theosophical Publishing House.

Theodore M. Ludwig. The Sacred Paths: Understanding the Religions of the World. Prentice-Hall, Inc., 2001.

Geddes MacGregor. Reincarnation in Christianity: A New Vision of the Role of Rebirth in Christian Thought. Quest Books, 1990.

Fr. Thomas Merton. The Seven Storey Mountain. Mariner Books, Anniversary Edition, October 1999.

Marvin W. Meyer and James M. Robinson. The Nag Hammadi Scriptures: The Revised and Updated Translation of Sacred Gnostic Texts. HarperOne, 2009.

Swami Muktananda, 'I am That: The Science of Hamsa from the Vijnana Bhairava. SYDA Publications:1978, 5th Edition.

_____. Play of Consciousness: A Spiritual Autobiography. Introduction by Gurumayi Chidvilasananda. SYDA Foundation, 2000.

Caroline Myss. Anatomy of the Spirit: The Seven Stages of Power and Healing. Harmony, 1997.

_____. The Different Paths of Buddhism: A Narrative-Historical Introduction. Rutgers University Press, 2005.

Paul Muller Ortega. The Triadic Heart of Shiva. State University of New York Press, 1989.

Sri Nisargadatta Maharaj. I am That, trans. Maurice Frydmein. Chetana, 1984.

Elaine Pagels. The Gnostic Gospels. Vintage, 1989. First copyrighted, 1979.

Raimon Panikkar. The Intra-Religious Dialogue. Paulist Press, 1999.

Patanjali. The Yoga Sutras. Swami Satchidananda, tr. Integral Yoga Publications, 1990.

Sw. Prakashananda. Cultivating a Peaceful World for Our Children. (article). Light On Light E-Magazine. Jan 2023.

Ram Dass. Remember, Be Here Now. Hanuman Foundation, 1971.

_____. Still Here: Embracing Aging, Changing, and Dying. Riverhead Books, 2001.

Richard Rohr. Immortal Diamond: The Search for our True Self. John Wiley and Sons, 2012.

Chogyam Trungpa Rinpoche. The Collected Works. Carolyn Gimian, ed. Shambhala, 2003.

Sakyong Mipham Rinpoche. Turning the Mind into an Ally. Foreword by Pema Chodron. Riverhead Books, 2003.

Sw. Satyananda Saraswati. Kundalini Tantra. Bihar School of Yoga, 1996.

Sw. Shankarananda. Consciousness Is Everything: The Yoga of Kashmir Shaivism. Shaktipat Press, 2000.

Shunryu Suzuki Roshi. Zen Mind, Beginner's Mind. Shambhala, 2011.

Lilian Silburn. Kundalini: The Energy of the Depths. Jacques Gontier, tr. State University of New York Press Series in the Shaiva Traditions of Kashmir, 1988. French edition, 1983.

Jaideva Singh. The Yoga of Delight, Wonder, and Astonishment: A Translation of the Vijnana-bhairava. Foreword by Paul Muller Ortega. State University of New York Press, 1991.

Sw. Shivom Tirth. A Guide to Shaktipat. Devatma Shakti Society, 1985.

Wayne Teasdale. The Mystic Heart. Foreword by His Holiness The Dalai Lama. New World Library, 1999.

Bri. Maya Tiwari. Path of Practice: A Woman's Book of Healing with Food, Breath and Sound. Ballantine. 2000.

Irina Tweedy. Daughter of Fire: A Diary of a Spiritual Training with a Sufi Master. The Golden Sufi Center, 1986 and 2006.

Llwellyn Vaughan Lee. The Face Before I Was Born: A Spiritual Autobiography. The Golden Sufi Center, 2009. First edition, 1997.

Christopher D. Wallis. The Recognition Sutras – Illuminating a 1000-Year-Old Spiritual Masterpiece. Mattamayura Press, 2017.

_____. Tantra Illuminated: The Philosophy, History, and Practice of a Timeless Tradition. Anusara Press, 2012.

Cornel West. African American Religious Thought. Westminster John Knox Press, 2003.

Walt Whitman. Leaves of Grass (poetry). Amazon, 2021.

Warren W. Wiersbe. Jesus in the Present Tense: The I Am Statements of Christ. David C. Cook, 2011. http://letusreason.org

Ken Wilber. No Boundary: Eastern and Western Approaches to Personal Growth. Shambhala, 1979 and 2001.

_____. The Essential Ken Wilber: An Introductory Reader. Shambhala, 1998.

Lama Yeshe. The Bliss of Inner Fire: Heart Practice of the Six Yogas of Naropa. Wisdom Publications, 1998.

Paramahansa Yogananda. Autobiography of a Yogi. Self Realization Fellowship, 1998.

_____. The Second Coming of Christ: The Resurrection of the Christ Within You. Self-Realization Fellowship, 2004. Two Volumes.

_____. The Yoga of Jesus: Understanding the Hidden Teachings of the Gospels. Self-Realization Fellowship, 2007.

Made in the USA
Monee, IL
21 January 2024

cc8ae43a-609e-432d-8a43-01629bb5449eR01